SCIENCE FAIR
HOW TO DO A SUCCESSFUL PROJECT

PLANTS

BY
JOHN M. LAMMERT

SERIES CONSULTANT
DR. JOHN M. LAMMERT
Associate Professor of Biology
Gustavus Adolphus College
St. Peter, Minnesota

**ROURKE
PUBLICATIONS
INC.**
Vero Beach, FL 32964
U.S.A.

LIBRARY OF CONGRESS CATALOGUING-IN-PUBLICATION DATA

Lammert, John, 1943–
    Plants / by John Lammert
        p. cm. — (Science fair)
    Summary: Suggests a variety of botany projects and experiments
suitable for a science fair.
    ISBN 0-86625-428-5
    1. Botany—Experiments—Juvenile literature. 2. Botany—Exhibitions—
Juvenile literature. 3. Plants—Experiments—Juvenile literature.
3. Science projects—Juvenile Literature.
[1. Botany—Experiments. 2. Plants—Experiments. 3. Experiments.
4. Science projects.] I. Title II. Series.
QK52.6.L36 1992
581' .078—dc20   92-4436
                                                                    CIP
                                                                    AC

DESIGNED & PRODUCED BY:
MARK E. AHLSTROM
(The Bookworks)

PHOTOGRAPHY:
Cover–COMSTOCK, INC.
Text–MARK E. AHLSTROM

TABLE OF CONTENTS

CHAPTER 1.
What Makes A Science Project "Scientific?" 4
CHAPTER 2.
Choosing Plants As A Topic For Your Project . . 8
*What types of projects can you do
about plants?* 10
CHAPTER 3.
Planning Your Project 19
Stating your purpose 19
Gathering information 19
How an investigation is done 22
CHAPTER 4.
Doing Your Project 30
Safety 30
Keeping a record 31
Coming to conclusions 33
CHAPTER 5.
Presenting Your Project 34
Making graphs to show your data 34
Putting your display together 38
Your written report 40
Judging of your project 41
Final words of encouragement 43
SOURCES OF SUPPLIES 44
GLOSSARY 45
INDEX 48

CHAPTER 1

What Makes A Science Project "Scientific?"

In a good science project, you will be an investigator. You will look at clues provided by the world about you and will make some sense of them by planning and doing an experiment. This is what scientists do when they observe some natural phenomenon and want to investigate it—they use the **scientific method**. In an organized fashion, scientists follow a series of steps that are designed to help them come up with an explanation for something they have observed.

When scientists observe something new, they wonder "How can that be?" The scientists have identified a problem. A scientist then makes an educated guess, or a **hypothesis**, that might explain the observation or solve the problem. It is "educated" because the scientist has some knowledge of the subject matter or reads what other scientists have found out through their experiments about the problem.

Steps Followed in the Scientific Method

✔ Make an *observation*.

✔ State the problem: What do you want to find out?

✔ What is already known about the observation?

✔ Develop a *hypothesis*: What do you think is a reasonable explanation for the observation?

✔ Design an *experiment* that will provide answers: What materials will be needed and how will they be used?

✔ Record *data* or observations: What happened during the experiment?

✔ Analyze the results.

✔ Come to a *conclusion*: What did you learn? Did your data support your hypothesis? What do your results mean?

Let's look at an example of an observation and a hypothesis. From this observation, a hypothesis will be made.

Have you noticed that a house plant near a window will have a long stem that grows toward the light? This happens because plants need light for **photosynthesis**, the process by which plant cells use the sun's light energy to turn carbon dioxide and water into sugar and oxygen.

This plant bends toward the light from the window.

So, this house plant needs to get its leaves, where photosynthesis takes place, exposed to as much light as possible. Light from the sun is actually made up of different colors, all mixed together. A good question, then, might be "What color of light is best for growth of plants?" Since plants are green, you might guess that green light is the best color. Your hypothesis might be "Green light is best for plants to grow."

Next, the scientist makes a plan to test the hypothesis. This plan is called the **experimental design**. Materials are chosen and a series of steps are written out. Then the actual work can start.

Here is a possible experimental design for our hypothesis that green light works the best to attract plants. Young pea plants, or **seedlings**, growing in flower pots will be placed in boxes that have a large opening cut out of one side. Taped over each opening will be a piece of colored plastic—red, green, blue, and clear. The box with the clear plastic is called a **control** because it will let in light of all colors. Another control box will have no opening for light to enter. Each box will have five pea seedlings. The boxes will be placed by a window to receive at least eight hours of daylight each day.

Then the actual work can start. The seedlings are grown and the boxes are built. When the seedlings are ready, they are placed in the boxes and the experiment begins.

The seedlings in this box are exposed to green light only.

During the experiment **data** are collected. This means that what you see and measure is recorded. In our example, the seedlings in each box are checked for growth each day for a week. The height of each plant and the distances between their leaves are recorded. The color of each plant is written down. Anything unusual is also noted. If our hypothesis is right, the plants in the green box will grow just like the plants that get complete light. Plants in the other boxes should grow differently.

The **results** are studied. Here are some things to look at. What were the color of the leaves in each group? Did the seedlings bend the same way or differently? How long were the stems in each group? How did the plants grown in the dark compare with the other plants?

Finally, from these results, **conclusions** are made. What was learned? Was the hypothesis correct? If it was not correct, then what would be another hypothesis? What do these data mean about the life of a plant?

The scientist will then use these data to make some **predictions** that will lead to more experiments. When the data from an experiment have been studied, there are often new questions that require answers. A scientist doesn't stop doing experiments even after winning the Nobel Prize!

CHAPTER 2

Choosing Plants As A Topic For Your Project

What makes a good science project? Students with experience will probably tell you that the hardest part is finding a topic. Take plenty of time trying to think of a good topic. This book is written to help you decide what to do. It's important that you are interested in the topic you choose. This means that you will be excited about what you are doing. You usually learn better when you are excited about something. Don't think you must have a difficult project, especially if this is your first. The best projects often focus on something simple.

As a subject for a science fair project, plants have many things going for them. You might think that plants are boring, but they offer much to investigate. As living organisms, plants respond to their environment. They are affected by light, heat, moisture, and chemicals. They heal in response to injury. Some plants even communicate with each other! Plants are important to each of us. They provide us with clothing, foods, healing drugs, and oxygen. We can build homes because of plants. We plant flower gardens for their beauty. Plants also provide habitat for animals. Unlike animals, however, you don't have to clean up after them.

This book will guide you through the basic steps you need to follow so you can complete a successful science project about plants. In the next few pages you will read about project ideas that focus on plants. You will not find step-by-step instructions. Instead, the ideas are here to spark your imagination and to turn on your creative powers. That's what makes science fun—imagination and creativity.

Plants make life more beautiful.

What types of projects can you do about plants?

There are three different types of projects you can choose to do about plants:

☆ You can prepare an *exhibit* that displays a collection or shows what you learned after reading about plants.

☆ You can do a *demonstration* of a lab experiment you found in a book.

☆ You can do an *investigation* that uses the scientific method to explore a problem.

Sometimes science fair rules discourage the first two types of projects. Teachers or judges may feel that these projects are not scientific enough. However, you might be able to do an exhibit or demonstration *if* you add a little investigation to the project. It's a good idea to have your teacher go over your project plans with you. This will help you find out if your project satisfies your local rules.

☞ *Exhibits*

Botanists (scientists who study plants) often look at plants to discover how they are alike or different. Take a look at the leaves on trees, bushes, and garden plants in your neighborhood. You will see that the leaves differ in their shapes and where they grow along a stem. Botanists use this knowledge to identify plants and to see if some plants are related to each other. The arrangements and colors of flowers are also used to place plants into related groups. So you might prepare an exhibit that displays a leaf or flower collection of plants in your neighborhood. You could collect leaves or flowers from plants that all grow in a meadow, or in the shaded part of a forest, or in the desert, or by the ocean. A library will have guidebooks to help you identify plants by looking at their leaves or flowers. Be sure to check if it is legal to remove leaves or flowers from plants where you plan to collect. Get permission if you go on private property.

Plants use various ways to spread seeds from the "mother" plant so new plants will grow. Seeds can have feathery parachutes or wings so they move with the wind. They can have tiny hooks that attach the seeds to an animal's fur. Where a plant grows is related in part to how its seeds are spread. You could collect different kinds of seeds and explain how they are spread.

Seasonal differences can be observed among wild flowers. As the seasons change from spring to summer to autumn, different wild flowers appear, show their colors, form seeds, and then die. An exhibit could be prepared that shows this seasonal parade of wild flowers from a nearby woods. If you live in a desert, there is a beautiful display of wild flowers that pop out after a rain.

A meadow is filled with colorful wildflowers in the spring of the year.

An exhibit could be made that shows the main parts of flowers and explains what each part does. Such a project should show some imagination in its construction. Flowers are built so the plant can release pollen and take on pollen from other plants. For some plants, the wind moves pollen from one plant to another. In other plants, pollen is carried on the bodies of insects, or even bats! Carefully drawn illustrations that show these flower features is one way to do this type of project. Don't tear pictures out of magazines or books. Photocopies of pictures found in books don't look good in an exhibit.

Plants have been used for centuries to treat human diseases. Native Americans chewed willow bark to treat headaches and fever. Guess what was in the bark—a drug that is related to aspirin! People sick with malaria are sometimes treated with a drug called quinine. Quinine is found in the bark of a South American tree called chincona. For hundreds of years people in Peru drank a tea made from the bark of this

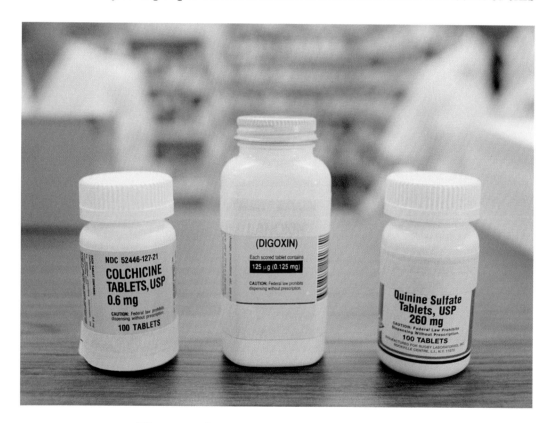

These medicines are made from plants.

The aloe plant is used by some people to help heal a burn.

tree to cure malaria. Gardeners have long liked to plant the purple foxglove because of its beautiful thimble-shaped flowers. Almost 2000 years ago a tea made from foxglove leaves was used to treat the disease called dropsy. This disease occurs when a heart doesn't beat strongly enough. Today, a drug called digitalis is extracted from foxglove leaves and used to treat this heart disease. Drug companies keep searching throughout the world for old remedies that use plant materials to treat human diseases. You could do an exhibit that features some of these medicine-producing plants and the diseases they cure.

☞ *Demonstrations*

The library may have some books that describe how to do some experiments that investigate plants. Sometimes these are too simple and only take a short time to do. If you decide to do one of these easy projects, it will probably receive a low rating by your teacher or science fair judge.

Here are some demonstrations that you might do:

❀ Some plants inhibit the growth of other plants.

❀ Some plants make substances that kill insects which damage vegetables growing in a garden.

❀ Hydroponic gardening—a way to grow plants without soil.

After you read the next section, put on your thinking cap and see if you can add something to a demonstration that will make it an investigation.

☞ *Investigation*

The best type of science project shows an investigation that you carried out. By exploring some feature of plants in an investigation project, you will learn more about how scientists think and work. You will also learn some important things about the world around you.

Let's review again the questions you need to ask as you plan and carry out a project that uses the scientific method:

❀ What do you want to find out? This is the *problem* that you have decided to investigate.

❀ What is already known about the problem?

❀ What is your experimental design for an experiment that will give you an answer to your problem?

❀ What do you think will happen? This is your *hypothesis*.

❀ What did you observe happen? These *observations* are written in your lab notebook.

❀ Analyze your data.

❀ What did you learn from the observations? Did you find that your hypothesis was correct? If not, can you think of another hypothesis? These are your *conclusions*.

Here are some suggestions for a question to ask about plant biology. These problems focus on the effect of different things on seeds, seedlings, plants, or **algae** (*al GEE*):

What is the effect of _____ on _____?

Fill in the first blank space with an item you choose from the first column below. Fill in the second blank space with an item you choose from the second column below.

Column 1	Column 2
✿ different colors of light (red, green, blue versus white)	✿ **germination** of seeds
✿ different brightnesses of light	✿ growth of seedlings
✿ different temperatures	✿ growth of plants
✿ household chemicals like sugar, salt, baking soda, cleaning solutions[*]	✿ growth of algae
✿ aspirin[*]	
✿ different amounts of detergent	
✿ different fertilizers	
✿ different amounts of a fertilizer	
✿ different sounds	
✿ different kinds of music	
✿ different loudnesses of sound	
✿ acidity (use different concentrations of vinegar)[*]	
✿ an electromagnetic field[*]	
✿ cigarette smoke[*]	
✿ different types of soils (use sand, clay, vermiculite, loam, etc.)	

[*] *Do only with adult supervision*

15

Column II lists algae, plants that you may not have heard about. They are simple plants. Some of them grow as "green scum" along the edges of a pond or lake. Others are hair-like and are attached to rocks in streams. Sometimes green algae grow in aquariums that have not been cleaned. If you live by an ocean, the brown seaweed you find on the shore are a type of algae. They can be seen growing on rocks in the pools that form when the tide goes out.

Algae grow as green scum along the edge of this stream.

Maybe you can think of something else to test for its effect on plants or seeds. Science can be more fun when you use some imagination in designing an experiment.

Here is a list of other problems about plants about which you could design an experiment:

✿ What are the effects of gravity on the roots and growing tips of corn and oat seedlings?

✿ Can you create an artificial gravity that will influence plant growth, by growing seedlings on a slowly spinning phonograph turntable?

✿ What happens when you plant seeds of two different plants very close to each other and also plant the seeds several inches apart?

✿ Do seeds exposed to microwaves germinate faster or slower?

✿ Does soaking seeds for different lengths of time affect their ability to germinate?

✿ How strong is a root as it grows out of a seed?

✿ Can light influence the direction a plant moves?

✿ How fast do different garden plants grow after their seeds have sprouted?

✿ Where does oxygen in the air enter plants—through the top side or bottom side of leaves, or through the stem?

✿ Which kind of fertilizer is better for growing plants—commercial plant food or homemade organic fertilizer?

✿ Are there differences in the numbers and types of **lichens** that grow where air pollution is high and where it is low?

You may have seen gray or orange, crusty-looking plants growing on large rocks or on tree trunks and not known what they are. Well, these are **lichens** (*LY kins*). These organisms are actually two kinds of things growing together. Algae and fungi cooperate so they can live together. The algae use photosynthesis to make sugar that the mold needs to grow. The fungi, in return, supply water and minerals to the algae.

In chapter 3, you will find some suggestions for which plants or seeds are good to use in a science project.

This rock is home to some lichens.

These science projects allow you to make predictions, something scientists want to do with the data they have collected. What is *most* important about the project you choose is that you are curious about it and involved with it.

CHAPTER 3

Planning Your Project

Stating your purpose

When you have finally picked a problem to study about plants, you then need to state the purpose of the experiment that you want to do. You can either make a statement or ask a question:

"The purpose of this project is to determine if pea seedlings will grow equally well in different colors of light."

or

"Are there some colors of light that are better for growth of pea seedlings?"

Notice that each of these sentences clearly states what the experimenter wants to find out. You should take some time to write a sentence that defines the problem you have decided to tackle. This will help make clear what you want to do during your investigation. The statement of your problem will be written in your *lab notebook*. Later in this chapter, you will learn more about this notebook and the "stuff" you should keep in it.

Gathering information for your project

☞ *The library*

The first place you want to visit to find information for your project is the library. This is where you will find books, encyclopedias, magazines, and newspapers with articles about plants.

The card or on-line computer catalog will tell you what books the library has. Look up the subject headings "Plants," "Botany," and "Science Experiments."

To find magazine articles about plants, use the *Readers' Guide to Periodical Literature.* There is a volume for each year. Look up the topic "Plants." For each article you will find the magazine's name, the volume number, and the pages on which the article appears. Ask the librarian for help if you need it.

Scientists use libraries a lot to find out what is going on in their area of interest. So this library search is good experience for a budding scientist.

As you read, it is important that you take good notes. Index cards (3 x 5 inches) work well. Don't write on scraps of paper. They are easily lost. Write down information that will help you organize your ideas and to plan the steps you will take to do your project. Each index card should include the author's name (if any); the name of the book, magazine, or newspaper; the date it was published; and the pages you read. Later, you will rewrite important index card information into your lab notebook.

Writing out note cards is a smart thing to do.

Use your own words when you summarize what a book or an article says. **Plagiarism**, that is, copying word-for-word, or changing just a few words here and there, is not proper behavior for any scientist. Teachers and science fair judges will not accept it. What you write on your display and in your report about your project *must be in your own words*.

☞ *"Plant People"*

Your community probably has several people who can give you some help on your plant project. A nursery, a garden supply center, or an **arboretum** will have people who know lots about plants. Many communities have a garden club. Your county may have an agriculture, conservation, or extension office. Your city or state may have a forestry service. Perhaps there is a college nearby where you will find a helpful botanist. Don't hesitate to get all of the information you can. The more you know, the better your project will be.

Scientists are easy to talk to.

21

How an investigation is done

☞ *Experimental design*

Once you have decided *what* you want to find out about plants, the next step is to decide *how* you will do it. You must decide what materials you need to use and what you will do with them. This is called the **experimental design**. In a scientific investigation, the answers to your problem should come from the experiments you plan.

A well-designed science project that investigates a problem about plants will be done under **controlled** conditions. This means that you intentionally change certain conditions to see how the seeds or plants respond. The conditions of an experiment that change are called the **variables**. You change the **independent variable** to see how the **dependent variable** changes. Here's another way of explaining these variables. The independent variable is something that you manipulate. The variable that responds to this manipulation is the dependent variable.

This may still be a little confusing. So, let's see how these terms apply to the experiment about the color of light and plant growth that was described in Chapter 1. In this experiment pea seedlings growing in boxes get their light only through a window covered with a piece of plastic. The independent variable (the variable that is changed on purpose) is the color of the plastic. The plants will be observed and measured to see how they grow when they get only light of a particular color. The dependent variable (the variable that responds to the change) is how much the plants grow in each box. The plants grown in these boxes with the colored plastic windows are called the **experimental groups**.

Control groups are also needed in an experiment. In the experiment on light color and pea seedling growth, one of the boxes has its window covered with clear plastic to let *all* light colors in. This is a control group. The other control group does not get any light. Any changes (the dependent variables) seen in the seedlings grown in the presence of a single light color (the independent variable) are compared to those in the control boxes. These changes could be the height and color of the pea seedlings.

To make sure that any changes in plant growth are due *only* to a particular color of light, other things must be controlled. This means that all boxes must have the same number of plants that are grown in the same type of container, in the same potting soil, at the same temperature, and with the same amount of water. To receive the same amount of light, the boxes are placed so that sunlight or a plant growth lamp shines evenly on all the box windows. You might come up with some other conditions that must be the same for all groups.

A mistake made by many beginners is to use too few plants. If you used only one plant in each group and one plant died, what does that mean? Did your treatment kill the plant, or did you forget to water it, or did you give it too much water? There's no way to tell. So, use *at least* five plants in each group.

It's a good idea to ask your teacher, parent, or other knowledgeable adult to check over your design. Let them make changes that might make the experiments safer or more practical. However, make sure that the plan is *your* plan.

Measurements are carefully written down in a lab notebook.

☞ *Lab Notebook*

You will need a lab notebook in which to write down everything about your experiment. This includes what you want to find out and what your guess, or hypothesis, is for the outcome of the experiments. The notebook also contains a list of the materials you use and how they are used. You record what you observe or measure. You write down what you think the data you collected means. You list all of the sources you used to gather information to help you in the project. This includes people, books, and magazines. The first page will have the project's title, followed by your name, grade, and school. A table of contents at the beginning will help readers find the different parts of the project.

The lab notebook could be a spiral-bound notebook or a three-ring binder. It should be used only for your science project. Remember to write everything down in this book—don't use scraps of paper. The notebook does not have to be real neat, but your handwriting should be clear enough so other people can read your ideas. Your teacher and science fair judges will look at it.

☞ *Materials*

The things that you will use for your plant project must be chosen with care. These might include seeds or plants, pots for growing them, soil, fertilizer or other chemicals, a light source, and measuring tools. The list of materials must be *exact*. It states *what* and *how much* will be needed to do the project.

Seedlings listed in the table on the next page are good choices if you decide to study the effects of chemicals, light, or gravity. Seeds for a mustard plant (Wisconsin Fast Plants™) that grows rapidly are available from the Carolina Biological Supply Co. (see the Appendix)

Seeds and plants for a project are easy to find. Good vegetable seeds include corn, radish, bean, and pea seeds. Flower seeds that grow fast include marigold, zinnia, and sweet pea. Seeds will germinate faster if they are soaked overnight with water and blotted dry with paper towels before they are planted. Radish, bean, corn, or pea seedlings are good choices. While it takes three to four weeks for these seedlings to grow big enough to do a project, the young plants are excellent subjects for an experiment. You might, instead, buy vegetable or flowering plants at a nursery. Then you won't have to wait for seeds to sprout and new plants to grow before you can start your project. Tomato and pepper plants are available in the spring at nurseries and gardening departments. Grasses can be used if you are interested in observing the effects of pollutants on road-side plants. However, don't limit yourself to these choices. You have the creativity to think of others.

Calendar for growing experimental seedlings

Plant seeds	Time needed to sprout	Time after sprouting when ready for experiment
Radish	7-10 days	10-14 days
Soybean	7-10 days	21-28 days
Kidney or Lima bean	5-9 days	14-21 days
Pea	7-9 days	7-18 days
Corn	7-9 days	7-18 days
Oat	3-4 days	7-14 days
Barley	3-4 days	7-14 days
Wheat	3-4 days	7-14 days
Wisconsin Fast Plant™	1 day	2-5 days

You should have little problem finding materials to be used in your plant project. Nurseries and garden supply stores in your community should have most of the items that you will need. Other sources are listed at the end of this book. If you want to buy something from a biological supply company, ask your teacher to place the order. Remember that it may take several weeks for the order to reach you, so begin to plan your work early.

☞ *Procedures*

The steps that you will follow in your experiment must be carefully organized. As you think about how you will do your experiment, write down each of the steps in the order they will be done. Include as much detail as possible. Your experimental design, or plan, should be written in your lab notebook.

A **flow chart** will help to remind you of the various steps that you need to follow in your experiments. This chart is a simple version of your experimental design. It reminds you what must be done next. Check off each step as you complete it.

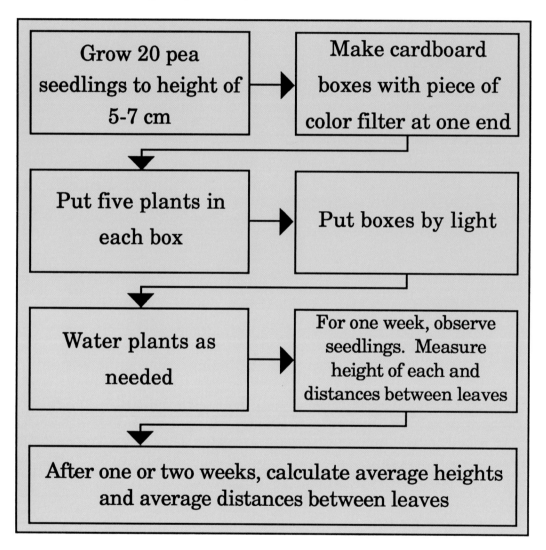

This is a flow chart for the experiment on light color and plants.

All of your measurements should use the metric system. Scientists all over the world measure length, volume, mass, and temperature in metric units. Measuring in metrics is easy because it is based on the number 10. This is just like American money. One dollar can be divided into into 10 dimes or 100 pennies. In the metric system, you will not have to worry about fractions. You will use decimals.

The basic metric unit for length is the **meter** (m). One meter is a little longer than one yard. A 100 yard football field measures 91.5 m. A meter is divided into 100 equal and smaller units called **centimeters** (cm). A meter is also divided into 1000 equal and still smaller units called **millimeters** (mm). Most rulers will have the metric scale printed on one side.

The basic metric unit of volume is the **liter** (l). One liter of lemonade is a little larger than one quart. A liter can be divided into 1000 equal and smaller units called **milliliters** (ml). A 12 ounce can of soda holds 296 ml. Measuring cups and medicine droppers can be used to measure amounts of liquids in milliliters. Your school might have graduated cylinders for measuring liquids.

The basic metric unit of **mass** is the **gram** (g). Mass measures the amount of matter, or "stuff," present in an object. Many people confuse mass with weight. Mass is not influenced by gravity as weight is. Large objects have their mass measured in **kilograms** (kg). One kilogram equals 1000 g. Some electronic kitchen scales will measure grams.

Temperature in the metric system is measured in degrees Celsius (°C). People who give the weather forecast on TV use the Fahrenheit (°F) scale. Water freezes at 0°C, or 32°F, and boils at 100°C, or 212°F. Body temperature is 37°C, or 98.6°F. A thermometer on a nice spring day might read 25°C, or 77°F.

Metric System Symbols		
Length	**Volume**	**Mass**
meter = m	liter = l	gram = g
centimeter = cm	milliliter = ml	kilogram = kg
millimeter = mm		

Remember, it takes time to grow your plants.

☞ *Time schedule*

You should begin to plan your project several months before it is due. This will give you enough time to gather materials, do the project work, analyze the information you gather, write a report, and prepare a display. Estimate how much time each step should take and then add a little more time. Remember that seeds need from several days to over a week just to germinate. Seedlings usually need several weeks to grow large enough.

Here is a sample time schedule for an investigative project:

Week 1	- Choose a problem.
Weeks 2 and 3	- Gather information.
Weeks 4 and 5	- Plan your experiment and gather your materials.
Week 6	- Begin your experiment.
Week 7	- Continue to collect data from your experiment.
Week 8	- Finish data collection; begin to analyze data.
Week 9	- Prepare graphs; make display.
Week 10	- Practice oral report; science fair starts or project is due.

If you decide to grow your own plants, add at least three to four more weeks to this schedule.

You will have fewer hassles if you carefully plan a time schedule. This will help make sure that your project is finished in plenty of time before the science fair.

CHAPTER 4

Doing Your Project

Safety

"Safety first!" is the rule when working on a science project. Here are some tips to keep you from possibly being injured. A responsible adult should check your project plan for possible hazards.

Have a place of your own to work on your project. It might be a table in your classroom that your teacher assigns to you. The basement, garage, storage shed, porch, or your room at home is suitable as long as it is warm enough for the plants to grow. Keep your work area neat. As you do your project, be sure to clean up. Put away things that you no longer need.

If any chemicals are used in your project, use them *only* with an adult to supervise you. Wear protective glasses, rubber gloves, and a rubber apron. Wash your hands each time you finish using the chemicals. Keep your hands away from your mouth while you work. All chemicals should be clearly labelled and stored in a suitable container.

If your project requires that you go out into the woods, watch out for poisonous plants, like poison ivy. If the leaves of these plants touch your skin, it may get red and very itchy. To reduce the chances of getting these plant oils, as well as ticks, wear long-sleeved shirts and pants with legs. It may be a good idea to have an adult along when you visit a forest to collect.

Many plants have leaves, seeds, or fruit. Don't put any plant part in your mouth. If you touch plants, be sure to scrub your hands with soap and water right after you finish your work. If your project is a collection of plant leaves, seeds, flowers, or fruits, don't pick any of these unless you can identify the plant and know that it is safe to touch.

If you choose to study algae obtained from a lake or at the seashore, it may be a good idea to have someone come along who knows about water safety rules. Don't go wading in waters where the bottom is not familiar to you.

It's a good idea to have an adult with you
when you collect materials for your experiment.

Any electrical equipment should use batteries to power it. Electricity from a wall socket is too dangerous to use. Even though the current available from batteries is not strong, wires coming from them can become hot and thus possibly cause a burn.

Keeping a record

The lab notebook in which you wrote background information is also used to record your observations of the experiment. You can't write down too much! Don't expect to remember later what you saw or measured. Write down your measurements and observations *right away*!

There are two kinds of observations that you can record. A **qualitative** observation does not use measurements: "The plants grown under green light were shorter than the control plants." A **quantitative** observation uses measurements and numbers: "The

31

average height of pea seedlings grown under green light was four centimeters shorter than for plants grown with white light." Quantitative observations are more *precise*. Whenever possible, use quantitative observations for your project.

A scientist must be **unbiased** when observing what happens in the experiment. This means that you don't make the results come out the way you want them to. If the results are not turning out as you predicted, that's OK. Maybe your hypothesis is not correct. That's OK, too. An incorrect hypothesis means that you can rule out your "educated guess" as a possibility. Honesty is expected of scientists.

When you compare measurements of different groups, you will want to figure an *average* measurement for the plants in each group. It's a way to represent the measurements for all plants within a group. The arithmetic you use to compute an average is simple to do. Let's suppose that you are measuring the heights of pea seedlings grown under green light. These heights are added together. The sum is then divided by the number of plants in this experimental group. The answer from this last calculation is the average measurement for the group.

Data:	Calculating an average		
10.5 cm	10.5 cm	**11.0 cm**	The average
12.6 cm	12.6 cm	5⟌55.0	height of pea
11.0 cm	11.0 cm	5	seedling grown
11.5 cm	11.5 cm	5	under green
10.4 cm	10.4 cm	5	light is
	55.0 cm	0	**11.0 cm**

Photos of your germinating seeds or growing plants are one way to keep a record of your observations. These pictures should be clear. Make sure that your subjects are well-lighted. Hand-drawn illustrations that are neat can also be used.

Coming to conclusions

When you have completed your experiments, it is time to come to some conclusions. You did the experiment to get an answer to a question. Did your observations support your hypothesis? Explain everything in your lab notebook. If your data don't support your hypothesis, don't worry. Avoid stating that the experiment was a "failure", or that it didn't work. Just explain what happened. Maybe some variable was not controlled. Go back over your notes in the lab notebook to find out where a mistake might have been made.

Most important in your conclusions is a statement of what your experiment means. For example, suppose that you find out that plants exposed to small amounts of a detergent do not grow as well as do control plants not exposed to detergent. You could then discuss how plants growing along polluted streams and rivers might be affected. Thus, your conclusions tie together what you found out from your experiment and the world in which you live.

Coming to conclusions takes lots of thinking.

CHAPTER 5

Presenting Your Project

Making graphs to show your data

Numbers you collected from your observations can be formed into **graphs**. Graphs will pack lots of information into a little space. They are a good way to present your data because they make it easier to understand the information. Paper on which to draw graphs can be bought at office supply departments. It comes with lines printed on the sheet. Use graph paper that has four or five lines per inch.

A **bar graph** can be made when you want to compare several groups. Bars may be drawn to represent the average amount measured for each group. A bar graph would be used to compare the numbers of individuals observed to have differing traits. To see how a bar graph can be made, let's use some data collected from an experiment. It shows the heights of pea plants grown at different temperatures for four weeks.

Group	Average Height
4°C (39°F)	5.1 cm
25°C (77°F)	11.5 cm
30°C (86°F)	18.3 cm
37°C (98.6°F)	21.4 cm

A line (the **horizontal axis**) is drawn at the bottom of the graph. This baseline has a place for each group. This line represents the independent variables, or the variables that you deliberately change. For our example, the independent variable is the temperature; the

34

temperatures have been intentionally chosen. The line on the graph's left side (the **vertical axis**) displays the amount of each dependent variable, or the measurement that changes in response to the change you cause. The average height of the pea plants in each group is the dependent variable in our example.

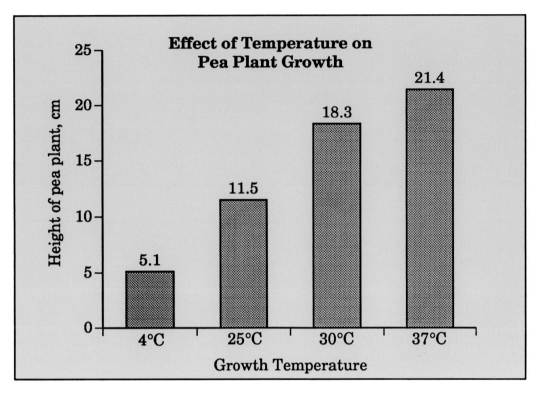

A bar graph compares data taken from groups.

Drawing a bar graph to show your data takes careful planning. A bar's height is proportional to an amount. Thus, you must decide how high each bar will be drawn on the graph paper. In our example, one cm on the graph paper represents five cm of average plant height. Choose how wide the bars will be—the bar widths must be the same. The bars can be drawn in different colors to make each group stand out.

A **pictograph** is constructed like a bar graph except that it uses a repeating symbol to represent the amount of an item. If there is a fraction in this amount, only a part of the symbol is used. The symbol you choose to use to represent an amount should have a simple shape that readers can easily recognize. As for a bar graph, you should plan a pictograph's layout. Decide how many symbols will need to appear in each row. Because you will use many copies of this symbol, all of them in the pictograph must look the same. There are several ways to do this. You could carefully draw your design and then make many copies on a copy machine. You could, instead, cut out your symbol from a piece of cardboard and then trace around the design.

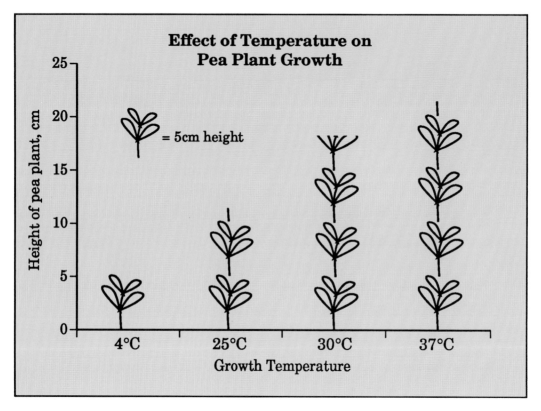

A pictograph is a type of bar graph.

A **line graph** uses a continuous line to show that the dependent variable in an experiment changes as the independent variable is changed. Frequently, a line graph shows how an experimental group changes over time. In these situations, time (minutes, days, weeks) is the independent variable, and so it is plotted along the horizontal axis. If you prepare a line graph that compares data taken from different experimental groups, the line for each group can be a different color.

Each graph must have labels on the left side and at the bottom. These labels are written so that the reader will know what the numbers represent. In addition, each graph must have a title that tells what observations are being shown.

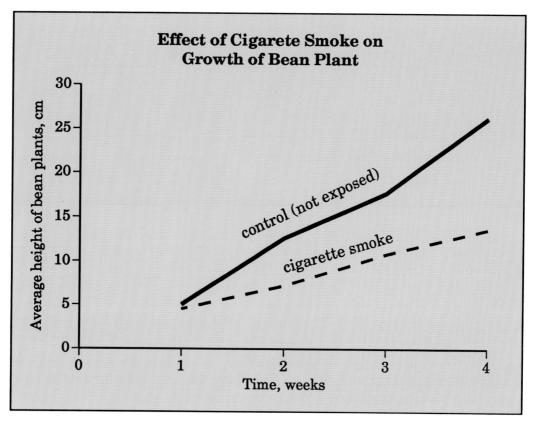

A line graph shows a change over time.

Lettering in a graph must be neat. You can use press-on letters purchased from an office supply store. Letters could be traced using a template. If you have access to a computer, it can be used to prepare a graph with proper labels.

Putting your display together

Visitors to your science project must be able to quickly understand what your project is about and what you did. A science project display tells a short story of your work on the project. It should show:

> ☆ A statement of the problem—what you wanted to find out.
>
> ☆ The hypothesis—how you guessed the experiment might turn out.
>
> ☆ Materials and methods—what materials you used and what you did with them.
>
> ☆ The results—what you observed.
>
> ☆ Your conclusions—did you find out what you wanted to know?

Science fairs usually have rules on the basic display design. Check with your teacher for local regulations, especially on the size of the space made available for you to show your project.

The most common display has three panels and stands by itself. Several sturdy materials are available for these panels. These panels can be made of ¼ or ⅜ inch plywood held together with hinges. The plywood can be painted or covered with cloth or paper. Foam board is lightweight, but strong enough to hold your written materials. Panels are easily cut out with a knife. Cloth tape can be used to make hinges that hold panels together. Foam board is available at office supply stores. Pegboard is also a handy material to use. It has holes already in it for hanging items. Because pegboard may bend if heavy objects are attached, you can nail 1" x 2" wood strips around the edges of the pegboard. Once these wood strips have been nailed on, hinges can be added. Some office supply stores and biological supply companies sell cardboard displays.

The center panel shows the project's title and some of the graphs you made from the data. Pictures of the experimental setup could be placed here instead of the graphs. On the left side, the statement of the problem and your hypothesis are shown. The right side can display any other results, as well as your conclusions. Each of these items is written or typed on a separate piece of paper.

Letters for the title can be cut from construction paper and should be at least two inches high. While neat hand printing is OK, your display will look better if you use a typewriter or word-processor for the other lettering. Since visitors to your display will stand several feet away, letters should be at least ¼ inch high. Be sure to have someone check the spelling, grammar, and punctuation in your display before you put it all together.

You might want to include drawings or photographs if they help explain your investigation. These illustrations need to be labelled.

How you attach materials to the display board is important. Staples look cheap! Tape hidden behind larger pieces is good. Test glues to find one that does not wrinkle paper after it dries. Before you fasten the pieces in place, lay everything out to see how it will look and fit on the display board.

Making a neat display is important.

Your written report

In addition to the lab notebook that was discussed in Chapters 3 and 4, some science fairs will expect that you prepare a written report on your project. This formally presents your work on the project. It shows readers the details of your efforts.

If possible, use a typewriter or computer. However, *very* neat handwriting is acceptable. The pages can be bound into a folder or a binder.

On the first page is the title of the project, your name, grade, and school. The table of contents is the second page. Readers can more easily find different sections if they know what pages to look up.   The

<table>
<tr><td>

Light Color
and
Plant Growth

Emily Johnson
Grade 6
North Elementary School
Petertown, Minnesota

</td><td>

Table of Contents
Statement of Problem........3
Background Research........4
Hypothesis.........................7
Experimental Design.........8
   Materials.......................9
   Procedures...................11
Data (Observations and
   Measurements...............13
Bibliography.....................16
Acknowledgments.............17

</td></tr>
</table>

statement of purpose explains why you wanted to work on this project about plants and what you wanted to find out about them. Included in the background research section are summaries of the articles and books you may have read (remember to use the notecards you made), the names and titles of the "plant people" to whom you may have talked, what you learned from them, and any other materials you found to help you plan your project.

The materials you used, how you used them, what data you obtained, and what the data mean are the next sections. The information you should include in these sections has been discussed earlier in this book.

The bibliography lists all articles and books you read. These materials are listed alphabetically by the authors' last names. Here are some examples to help you prepare a bibliography.

For a magazine:
Barinaga, Marcia. "The secret of saltiness." Science 254:664-665 (1991).

For a book:
Hodges, Laurent. Environmental pollution. New York: Holt, Rinehart and Winston, 1977.

Finally, you need to acknowledge all of those people who helped you on the project, thanking first those who gave you the greatest support and help.

Judging of your project

You will probably be expected to talk about your project to science fair judges or to your class. In four or five minutes you will have to:

- Introduce yourself, giving your name, school, and grade.
- Give the title of your project.
- Give the purpose of your project.
- Tell why you choose this project.
- Explain what you did.
- Show your results—explain any graphs or pictures that are in your display.
- Give your conclusions if you did an investigation project.
- Explain what you learned.
- Ask if there are any questions.

You can use notes to help remind you of what to say. However, if you practice several times, you won't have to look at them too often. Practice your talk while a parent, other relative, or a teacher listens. Ask this person for helpful suggestions.

When you finally give your talk, stand to the side of your display so the judge or other viewers can see your work. Talk slowly, even if you are really nervous! If you don't know the answer to a question, be sure to say you don't know. Remember, honesty is important.

The science fair judges who visit your display will evaluate your project for an award. Each science fair usually prepares its own judging sheet. However, most will score projects in these areas:

✔ Scientific thought - The judges will see if your project follows the scientific method. Has the problem been clearly stated? Are the procedures proper and thorough? Have controls been properly used?

✔ Creative ability - The judges will want to know how you chose this topic. Your score will be lower if you repeated something you read in a book or if someone else did the actual work. If a book, like this one, gave you the idea for your project, how did you use your imagination to develop the project more fully? More points will usually be given for scientific thought and for creativity than for the other areas.

✔ Understanding - Judges will ask some questions to see if you understand the key scientific features of your project. If you have prepared an exhibit, does the display provide some answers to questions about the topic?

✔ Clarity - The judges will examine your project to see if it clearly presents the hypothesis, procedures, data, and conclusions. Will the average person understand the project?

✔ Technical skill - Finally, the judges will check on how your display appears. Did you do most, if not all, of the work? How attractive is your display? Did you carefully check written materials for correct spelling and grammar?

Final words of encouragement

When you have presented your science fair project to your family, friends, and judges, feel good about what you have done. You have worked hard. You have become more aware of what scientists do. Science is "doing," not just memorizing some facts. You have learned how to find answers to a question about plants. By doing this project, you have discovered more of the wonder of science. Get fired-up and do another science fair project next year!

A good job is rewarded.

WHERE YOU CAN BUY SUPPLIES FOR PLANT EXPERIMENTS

Carolina Biological Supply Co.
2700 York Road
Burlington, NC 27215
1-800-334-5551 (East of the
  Rockies)
1-800-547-1733 (Rockies and
  West
1-800-632-1231 (North Carolina)

Connecticut Valley
  Biological Supply Co., Inc.
P.O. Box 326
Southampton, MA 01073
1-800-628-7748 (U.S.)
1-800-282-7757 (Mass.)

Edmund Scientific Co.
  (for color filters)
101 E. Gloucester Pike
Barrington, NJ 08007-1380
1-609-573-6250

EMD
A Division of Fisher Scientific
4901 W. LeMoyne Street
Chicago, IL 60651
1-800-621-4769
1-312-378-7770

Nasco
P.O. Box 901
Fort Atkinson, WI 53538-0901
1-800-558-9595

Science Kit &
  Boreal Laboratories
777 East Park Drive
Tonawanda, NY 14150-6784
  OR
P.O. Box 2726
Santa Fe Springs, CA 90670-4490
1-800-828-7777

Ward's
P.O. Box 92912
Rochester, NY 14692-9012
1-800-962-2660

GLOSSARY

algae - simple plants that usually grow in water. Green algae grow in the ocean, lakes, and soil, and on tree trunks. Brown and red algae grow in the ocean and are often called seaweeds.

arboretum - a place where trees, shrubs, and flowers are grown outdoors for educational purposes and for scientific study.

bar graph - a graph that uses columns to compare different values obtained for experimental groups. The height of each bar is proportional to the value.

botanist - a scientist who studies plants.

centimeter - the distance measured by 1/100 (0.01) meter. There are 2.54 centimeters in one inch (abbreviation: cm).

conclusions - what you interpret the results of an experiment to mean.

control group - a group in an experiment in which as many variables as possible are kept constant because they could affect the outcome of the experiment.

data - the observations and measurements that you make in an experiment.

dependent variable - the factor or condition that changes as a result of the presence of, or a deliberate change you make in, the independent variable.

experimental design - the plans you make so you can do an experiment. The design includes what you will use and how you intend to use them.

experimental group - a group in which all variables are the same as those in the control group *except* for the factor that you are following in your experiment.

flow chart - a list that is a shortened version of the steps you want to follow in doing your experiment. As you complete each step, you should check it off the list.

germination - the growth of a plant from a seed to a young plant with its first green leaves.

gram - the basic unit of mass in the metric system. There are 28.3 grams in one ounce (abbreviation: g).

hypothesis - a statement that gives a possible answer to a question. Because you may already know something about the question, a hypothesis is sometimes called an "educated guess." To see if it is true or not, a hypothesis is tested by doing an experiment.

horizontal axis - the line on a graph that goes across the bottom. It is used for showing values for the independent variable.

independent variable - the factor or condition that you want to study. In an experiment, you intentionally change this factor.

kilogram - the mass of 1000 grams. One kilogram is equivalent to about 2.2 pounds (abbreviation: kg).

lichen - crust-like or beard-like organisms that grow in unfriendly places like tree bark and rocks. They are formed from a close association of algae and molds. The algae provide sugar made from photosynthesis. The mold provides water and anchorage.

line graph - a graph that uses a line to see if the dependent variable changes as the independent variable is changed.

liter - the basic unit of volume in the metric system. One liter is a little smaller than one quart (abbreviation: l).

mass - the amount of matter, or "stuff," that is present. Weight is often confused with mass. Weight is the pulling force of gravity on matter.

meter - the basic unit of length in the metric system. One meter is a little longer (39.4 inches) than one yard (abbreviation: m).

milliliter - 1/1000 (one one-thousandths) of a liter. There are approximately 28 milliliters in one fluid ounce (abbreviation: ml).

millimeter - 1/1000 (one one-thousandths) of a meter. There are approximately 25 millimeters in one inch (abbreviation: mm).

photosynthesis - the process in which plants capture light to give them the energy needed to make sugar and oxygen from carbon dioxide and water.

pictograph - a graph that uses a series of pictures to show the values measured or observed for the dependent variables. It is put together like a bar graph.

plagiarism - copying word-for-word what someone else has written and not giving credit to that person.

prediction - what you think will happen in an experiment.

qualitative observation - an outcome of an experiment that is not an amount that can be measured, such as color.

quantitative observation - an outcome of an experiment that is measurable, such as numbers of individuals.

results - what you measure or observe as an experiment is carried out.

scientific method - a systematic strategy scientists use to discover answers to questions about the world. It includes making a hypothesis, testing the hypothesis with experiments, collecting and analyzing the results, and arriving at a conclusion.

seedling - a young plant. Usually the plant will have come up out of the soil about two to four weeks earlier.

unbiased - not allowing your preferences to interfere with collecting or analyzing data in an experiment.

variable - some factor in an experiment that can be changed.

vertical axis - the line on the left side of a graph. It shows the values of the dependent variables.

INDEX

Algae 15-17, 30
Average, calculating 32

Conclusions, coming to 33

Display 38-39
  construction 38
  lettering 39

Experimental design 6, 22-23
  variables 22
  controls 6, 22

Flow chart 26

Graphs, types of 34-37
  bar graph 34-35
  line graph 36-37
  pictograph 35-36

Judging 41-42
  talking to judges 41-42
  scoring of project 42

Lab notebook 23-24
Library, information in 19-21
  card or on-line catalog 19
  Reader's Guide to Periodical Literature 20
Lichens 17-18

Materials 24-25
Metric system 27

Notes, taking 20-21

Photosynthesis 5
Plants
  and medicines 12-13
  collections 10
  growing 24-25
  seeds 11
  Wisconsin Fast Plant 24, 25
Projects, types of 10-18
  demonstrations 13-14
  exhibits 10-13
  investigations 14-18
Purpose of investigation 19, 41

Record keeping 31-32
Report, written 40-41
Resource people ("Plant people") 21

Safety 30-31
Scientific method 4, 14, 42

Time schedule 29